Niina

*Memories of World War II by a Child Refugee Fleeing
from Estonia to Germany and Austria Eventually
Ending Up in Australia*

RITA REET DANKO

BALBOA.
PRESS
A DIVISION OF HAY HOUSE

Balboa Press books may be ordered through booksellers or by contacting:

Balboa Press
A Division of Hay House
1663 Liberty Drive
Bloomington, IN 47403
www.balboapress.com.au
1 (877) 407-4847

Print information available on the last page.

ISBN: 978-1-5043-0851-9 (sc)
ISBN: 978-1-5043-0852-6 (e)

Balboa Press rev. date: 05/26/2017

Dedicated

To my Mother whose heroism is the inspiration for this book.

Foreword

It took me twenty years of procrastination before I could write this book. A year before my Mother passed away she asked me to write her life story, I gave her a tape recorder with a tape in it and said, " here, talk." She did not like this, she wanted to talk but not to a lifeless tape, she wanted to talk to me. This was a bit of a problem as she lived in Sydney and I in Melbourne. I worked full time and still had children at home and a husband to take care of.

My Mother was eighty four years old and had an incurable disease. I knew I would need to hurry, time was running out so I visited her on many weekends flying from Melbourne to Sydney to hear her story. A story going way back to the time Estonia was enslaved by German Barons then independence for 20 years until Estonian Government was asked for bases by Stalin, the Soviet Dictator. Occupation followed by Russia, then Germany then Russia again and Second World War.

We had a war time history together, my Mother and I as we fled from Estonia in 1944, running from bombs raining down on Vienna from American bombers flying over us during the day and the British came to bomb at night. Hiding from Soviet soldiers when they occupied Austria and then ending up in Germany using people smugglers, only then they were called guides and they saved many lives including ours. We arrived in Australia in 1950 as war refugees and my own children were asking me for my story so I thought I could very well incorporate both, leaving a record of our ancestry and arrival in Australia for generations to come.

Ours is a turbulent story and I hope I can do it justice. My Mother's back ground story is mostly anecdotal as I was able to ascertain only some facts on various visits to Tallinn and Saaremaa in Estonia. Her story of Czar Nikolai 2nd of Russia and before is purely her, my Grandmother's personal stories and some historical data added by me.

My Mother passed away on 25th August 1995 and it took me twenty years before I could put her words onto paper. In the mean time I wrote four books on another topic, possibly in subconscious preparation for this book. At the time of writing there were media reports of refugees fleeing from war torn countries in 2015, just like we did many decades before. I actually saw them sleeping on hard concrete floors in Budapest railway station like my Mother and I slept in 1944 in Germany and that made me decide that now is the time or never.

I was in Hungary on a visit when the refugees were refused entry to Hungary and those that did make it over the border were not allowed for some time onto trains to travel further. Actually seeing their plight made me remember my promise to my Mother. Most people have no idea what it is like to sleep in a railway station where there are few toilets or running water, no nappies or milk for babies. No money even if there is anything to buy and the inhabitants are hostile. Even the space on concrete floor is limited as more and more people try to cram under cover for the night and there is always hunger. Not everyone in Budapest was hostile to the refugees, I saw many Hungarians bring food, drink and toys for the children. It was a very hot summer and the exhaustion, especially on the women's faces told many a story, also made me remember my own Mother's face on occasions as we fled from Estonia so many years ago.

My Mother is the bravest woman in the world. To venture across half the world with a small child in tow while the whole world was erupting at war, takes guts, strength of character, inventiveness, ingenuity, resourcefulness and also some luck. My Mother had all of it. She also had a soldier for a father who believed in discipline and endurance, He made her a very strong and brave woman whose story I hope I am able to do justice to.

He called her Niinushka when he was pleased with her, Niina, when he was not. The name on her legal documents is Maria but sometimes she also called herself Margot after her own mother whom she never knew.

She was born in St. Petersburg, Russia but her family history goes back further to the time Estonia was occupied by Germany and Estonians were Serfs on their own land.

Saga of the Long Black Coats

Juhan Tark took a wife and the whole village celebrated. The Baron on whose Estate he was a young serf, sent him a pig to roast, the band played and they all danced on the village square.

Suddenly, out of the night came a group of horsemen with whips lashing at the revellers. One of the horsemen rode straight to the bride, picked her up, sat her in front of his horse and back out into the night they all galloped. Juhan ran after them and was just in time to see the horsemen turn into the Baron's mansion. The Baron, Lord and Master of all the surround, took his right to the bride's first night.

Estonians were serfs on their own land, chattels of German Barons who owned everything. The Germans came as Traders and took all. Estonia is such a small country, together with Latvia and Lithuania, they are "The Baltic States." And have been occupied by one foreign country or another ever since the Vikings when they ruled the seas as far as the British Isles.

Juhan's bride returned after a week. Juhan did not speak and she only cried. After nine months a child was born, they called her Anna. The Baron made Juhan an overseer of his serfs and gave him land. The other serfs knew why and envied him but Juhan grew more and more morose, sullen and angry. Time went and Anna grew into a young lady. She was always welcome at the Baron's mansion and he taught her to read and write.

One day a young German friend by the name of Triipman was visiting the Baron. Anna spent more and more time at the Baron's house and became friends with Triipman. After Triipman left back to Germany, Anna discovered she was pregnant and in time gave birth to a daughter she called Margot. The Baron invited Anna and Margot to stay in his mansion and when Margot was 14, sent them both to Petrograd in Russia, ruled by Czar Nikolai 2nd at the time. Margot to attend school and learn etiquette to find a good husband, Anna went as her chaperon. After two years of learning the finer art of setting tables, cook, budget and decorate, she was deemed to be ready to attend the ball organised at the Czar's palace each year for debutants. At the ball she was noticed by an officer from the Czar Regiment and he asked Margot for a dance. Afterwards he asked Anna if he could visit them.

Officer Pahvel Salnikov was one of Czar Nikolai's body guards, much older than Margot but deemed to be a good catch. He asked Anna for Margot's hand in marriage, they accepted and Anna moved permanently in with them to a Dacha just out of Petrograd or St. Petersburg as it was also called. My mother was born to Margot and Pahvel on 12th December 1911. They called her Maria.

In the meantime in Estonia there was a revolution. It was a general uprising of the serfs and the German Baron's mansions and villas burned all over Estonia. The serfs donned long black coats because they were less visible wearing them as they stealthily moved through the night to loot, burn and kill. It was their only weapon against the soldier's guns guarding the Barons, these long black coats made them almost invisible at night as they silently moved to eliminate the soldiers one by one.

Juhan lead his men to the Baron's mansion. They were about thirty strong, all wearing long black coats. The soldiers guarding the mansion did not see them until it was too late, their rifles were useless in close combat and those that were not killed, fled into the night.

They opened all the stable doors and let the animals loose, then torched the stables. Juhan's men wanted to torch the Baron's mansion also but Juhan said, "Lets find him first and string him up" but the Baron and his household had already fled. Juhan and his men emptied the mansion of all food from the kitchen, the cellar of wine, and the mansion of all the riches they had helped to amass and then watched as the empty house went up in flames.

Still, this was not enough for Juhan, he wanted revenge. He was not alone, all Estonia wanted revenge. Revenge for the years of labouring as serfs on their own land and making the Barons rich from their sweat, for stolen brides, beaten and dead friends, torture and loss of self -respect.

Estate mansions were burning all over Estonia that night and "The Long Black Coats" were rejoicing.

Someone discovered that all the German Barons who were unable to escape by ship had fled into the nearby fortress. The Serfs surrounded the fortress and told the Germans to come out and if they left Estonia, they would not lift a sword against them. When the Germans were all out of the fortress the serfs surrounded them and stoned them to death, keeping their word not to lift a sword against them. After all, they had no swords and the Germans forgot that swords were weapons of the gentiles.

"Moisad polevad,
Saksad surevad,
Eestimaa on mejjede."

"Eesti folksong"

The serfs were illiterate and their important events were recorded for posterity in song and rhyme, including the "Saga of The Long Black Coats."

Anna Salemaa

There was also an uprising in Russia. The Czar and his family were arrested by the Bolsheviks and many white Russians, Royalists, high placed officials and Officers had already fled to Paris and their properties confiscated. Salnikov's young wife Margot wanted to follow her friends to Paris but Salnikov was in favour of going to Estonia since his mother-in-law had property there and some assurance of security for their future. No compromise was reached. The young wife Margot, my Grandmother left for Paris one night, leaving her child, Mother and husband behind. She was never heard of again.

February, 1917 there was mutiny at the gates of the Winter Palace as the soldiers disobeyed the order to shoot at the workers and women who came to protest peacefully calling, "STOP THE WAR, FEED THE CHILDREN. The soldier's mutiny the encouraged the Generals to abandon the Czar. Czar Nikolai the 2nd of Russia promptly abdicated and was arrested with his whole family by the Bplshevics, later sent to Siberia where they were all killed.

Russia was still at war with Germany and Salnikov fearing for his own life now the Czar was arrested dressed himself, his Mother-in-law and young daughter Maria as peasants, harnessed a horse and sleigh from his stable and made the long trek to Estonia. When the horse was confiscated by soldiers they walked through the snow.

The land in Estonia that Anna had given to her by the Baron, was confiscated when Estonia became a free and independent country but Anna had three half -brothers inheriting Targa Juhan's land in Merikula, Narva that was not confiscated. One of the brothers had drinking debts and was happy to sell some of his land to Anna. Salnikov married his mother in law Anna, so as to be able to stay in Estonia and she became my Grand-mother as well as my Great Grand-mother, Mother and Grand-mother to my mother.

Salnikov did not approve of the Estonian school system for his daughter, my Mother, deeming it inferior to Russia especially since his daughter was expelled from a few schools for fighting. He decided to teach his daughter all she needed to know at home. As a soldier, he knew of nothing else but to bring her up as a soldier, under strict discipline. My Mother became very strong and tough, speaking Russian and German fluently, French and English passably and she had a wide knowledge of history, geography, politics and strategy. This knowledge was very useful in later life during our flight from Estonia.

Salnikov, an officer did not work, he left the farming to his new wife, Anna and spent most of his days at the Russian Officer's Club in Tallinn. There, he was picked up together with all the other Russian elite officers, by the Bolsheviks when they occupied Estonia and he was deported to Siberia, never to be heard of again. His wife, my Great Grandmother promptly Estonianised her name from Salnikov to Salemaa so she would be spared the same fate. Computers were unheard of at the time and changing names was not uncommon, war and fire was often the cause of lost ID papers, especially when politically warranted and it was easy to change a name.

My Grandmother was a great story teller, and we children would spend many a cold dark night sitting in front of the huge fireplace eagerly listening to life in the Palace at St. Petersburg.

All the balls they would attend, the glittering chandeliered gold decorated halls and parquetted floors they would glide on, gloriously gowned and bejewelled women, handsome men in white uniforms and fascinating gossip of life so different from ours.

I remember clearly one of her stories because it was so bizarre. It was the time she had tea with the Czarina and her ladies at court. I was fascinated by the tale of a "taster" assigned to the Czarina. Everybody had to wait until the taster had tasted the food and drank the tea before they all did. Poison was the preferred method of assassination at the time. I always wondered what would happen if the taster fell dead and pitied the Czarina because her tea would always be cold.

The samovars at court were of decorated porcelain from a famous manufacturer in Dresden, Germany. Samovars were modern day water urns only more show pieces. The teapot with tea would sit on top of it and the whole thing was covered by a babushka doll with a huge quilted skirt to keep everything warm. Tea would be served in glasses sitting in an ornate silver holder.

Grandmother also delighted to talk about the gold and jewels she sewed into her coat and dress hems before leaving Russia, a fortune which made their road to Estonia easier and allowed Salnikov a life of ease at the Russian Officer's Club in Tallinn, also bought the house and piece of land in Merikula. Anna was not much older than Salnikov and he married her so as to be able to stay in Estonia.

I fondly remember the house that came with the land in Merikula. It was a small house built from stone found in the area with a shingle roof on top. Stone houses were unusual for country dwellings in Estonia at the time and most of them were built from wood. The windows were small to keep the cold out and the warmth in and the walls were as thick like a fortress. An apple orchard was next to the house and beyond that stretched a birch tree forest. A road through the forest took you to a clearing that ended as a steep cliff down into the Baltic Sea. My sister and her friends found a way down the cliff to go swimming in summer but I was never allowed to go, too dangerous I was told. I went with Grandmother to pick berries or mushrooms in the forest instead. A meadow with colourful wild flowers surrounded the house and grandmother's cows and sheep often grazed on it. I remember rolling in the delightful smelling long grass.

When the weather became colder I would wake up every morning, run to the window and see if snow had fallen, eventually to be rewarded with frost encrusted, star patterned windows and vistas of white blanketed snow covering the entire landscape outside. Later, icicles would hang from the low roof and Grandmother would shear them off with a spade so they would not injure us by falling. I loved to pick up the icicles and throw them like spears at the barn wall or suck them like cold, watery lollypops. I remember going on toboggan rides with my sister. I did not mind pulling her as she sat on the toboggan, I could always jump on whenever we came to a hill and I knew where many of them were.

My parents worked in Tallinn which was about two hours train ride away and my sister and I spent much time with Grandmother in the country.

Tallinn, Estonia

I have lived a charmed life. I am sure angels were watching over me as World War 2 jack booted over Europe causing immeasurable chaos throughout, separating families, destroying cities and homes, killing thousands of people and creating lots of refugees wandering the earth looking for a safe haven. I know what it was like as I and my Mother became displaced persons, constantly on the move, constantly apprehensive, fearful, hungry, cold and homeless. Like hunted animals, running to escape harm from bombs, guns and shrapnel. I was only six years old but I distinctly remember the noise, fire and fear that aeroplanes evoked, aeroplanes that rained fire, noise and death.

I was born in Tallinn, Estonia and had everything anyone could ask for, a nice home, family and plenty to eat. I was a healthy, happy, obedient child I was told, never sick or temperamental. In contrast to my older sister who was often sick, screaming for attention and a tiny sniffle from her would send my Mother and Grandmother to call for the doctor. My sister got all the attention from everyone leaving me to wish that I could be sick too. She had her own plate, cup, cutlery and a personal hen who laid eggs only for her, I was not allowed to touch any of her things nor, heaven forbid drink or eat from her dishes. Nevertheless, I did. It gave me great pleasure to stealthily take her cup and drink from it, even lick her spoon. Only later did I discover that my sister had tuberculosis which was highly contagious and I was so lucky not to have contracted it.

I always tried to join my sister and her friends. They played jokes on me, running away or hiding and consequently I became a loner. I had imaginary angels as company and years later a physic painter painted me an angel she saw around me which uncannily corresponded to the face of one of the imaginary ones I kept company with as a child.

We spent many glorious summers at Merikula, my Grandmother's farm. She also had a small house in Tallinn, Kadriorg, Roheline aas 14. Close to this house was a beautifully kept public park, well-kept expanses of green grass and lots of colourful flowers. I remember the strict rule, never to step on the grass or pick any flowers. A lake was in the middle of this park and white swans swam there with their young ones in tow.

Kadriorg is about 2 kilometres out of Tallinn in a green belt with many different parks. My favourite was a forested park where squirrels played, scampering up and down the tall trees. Lots of people always walked there and our President had his residence there as well. Nearby was a castle built for the Russian Czarina's proposed visit to Estonia. She never came and the palace was converted into an art museum. Years later visiting Estonia I walked up the staircase of this same palace, now museum and was suddenly transported back into my childhood, seeing myself crawling up these stairs on hands and knees and one stair creaked at exactly the same place as it did then. On top of the stairs were sombre, dark, paintings of angry looking men on the walls, they looked down on me and one of them had eyes that followed me around everywhere I went. I felt like I was being watched by a painting.

My Parents had an apartment in the centre of Tallinn just as you enter through the two towers leading to the ancient walled city of Reval. I could see the flower sellers sitting beside the fortress wall from the upstairs window and there were always lots of people walking the old cobble stones. Glimpses of high buildings from the new city towering above the fortress wall were just visible but my interest was with the flower sellers and their customers. I became very familiar with this view from the window. Below, in the courtyard was the back entrance of a movie theatre called "Bibabo Kino." The name fascinated me and I loved to watch the people exiting through the back yard after a movie. Being in the city was a treat as both my Parents worked. I was mostly with Grandmother in Kadriorg or in the country at Merikula.

My Father's family came from Saaremaa, the largest island near to mainland Estonia. The story goes that a French sailor by the name of Ravel jumped ship at Saaremaa a hundred years ago, found the island good and stayed there becoming our ancestor. The only industry on the island was fishing but at the time of Prohibition it was easy for fishermen to become smugglers between Finland and Estonia. Smuggling alcohol was a profitable business and my Father's family profited handsomely, eventually moving to mainland Tallinn where they bought and operated a stone quarry nearby.

My Father, Viktor was the youngest of three boys in the Raavel family, William and Johannes the other two. They were well known socially in Tallinn and my Father was engaged to be married to a beautiful, tall, blue eyed blonde. (My Aunt Adele, William's wife told me many years later). A group of them were at a dance when there were angry words between Viktor and his blonde fiancée and Viktor was heard to say in a loud voice to her and everyone else.

"You are not the only woman in the world, I can marry the next girl that enters the dance hall." And his fiancé shouted. "Go ahead, I dare you."

The door opened and in stepped my Mother. She was small,

dark and pretty but apparently nothing like my Father's fiancée. Viktor went up to this small dark woman, asked her for a dance and soon after they were married. I arrived nine month later. My Mother already had Jungle, my sister who was four years older than I. Jungle was my sister's name. Phonetically it sounds quite different from the way it is pronounced in English. Apparently my Mother read a book and Jungle seemed an exotic name for a girl. I was given the historic Estonian name, Reet. I don't think my Parents were happy, my Father's Parents certainly were not and going by what I heard later from Aunt Adele, my Mother was ostracised by the family especially after she introduced my sister to them as her dowry. This was 1937, my Mother was a very brave woman indeed. I have no memory of my paternal Grandparents, so obviously we were not welcome there.

My Father

Estonia was occupied by Soviet forces prior to World War II. After the war broke out, we were liberated from the Soviets by Germany, they in turn were eventually driven out and Estonia together with the other Baltic States, Latvia and Lithuania were again conquered by the Soviets who then remained and occupied Estonia for the next 44 years.

My Father was forcefully mobilised into the Soviet army the first time the Soviet army occupied Estonia and I remember very little of him. The two images etched into my mind are one, where he is sitting on a swing in Grandmother's garden at Kadriorg and I am sitting on his lap. I remember the sleepy comfortable warmth as he pressed me close to his chest and his gentle voice went on and on. I do not know what he said; I just remember the feeling of safety, warmth and love.

Next memory of my father is early on a wet, cold morning with my Mother and Grandmother, we stand on the rocky beach of Pirita silently waiting togetherwith many other women when a long queue of men comes marching up the beach and there, one of the men is my Father. I call out "Daddy, Daddy." My Father stops, turns around and looks at me. Next moment a soldier runs up, hits my father with the end of his rifle and shouts, "davai." My Father does not look back again but gets up from his knees and marches on with the others. The long queue of men marches to rowing - boats waiting to take them to the large ship further out at sea. I never see my father again as he gets lost amongst so many men all marching to the ocean. I remember being scared when my Father was clubbed by the soldier yet angry at the same time. My anger punctuated by the force of ocean waves crashing against rocks in the stormy sea, again and again.

My attention was then diverted to a woman on the beach giving birth, her knees spreading the rocks apart as her body convulsed pressing her deeper into the sand. Her screams echoed by the seagulls as they flew off in the direction of the boats labouring towards their destiny.

Soldiers came and soldiers went. My sister and I were mostly at my Grandmother's farm in Merikula and much of the internal turmoil passed us by. I know that soon after my Father was mobilised into the Soviet army, German soldiers drove the Soviets out and many in Estonia were jubilant. Germans were much preferred to the Russians.

After a while, life was good again until one day without warning the Kindergarten at Kadriorg which I attended, was bombed. Not only the Kindergarten but all of Tallinn was under Soviet air attack. I was suddenly forcibly lifted into the air and deposited against something hard. I must have lost consciousness then, as I only remember opening my eyes and finding it hard to breathe, there seemed to be a lot of smoke and screams. Panic surged in my chest and up my throat as I found myself pinned under and covered with rubble, it was so hard to move. Then, I saw a small hole of light in the distance and instinctively knew I have to get out from under this rubble as quick as I can. How I made it out into the open I have no idea but when I did the world around me had changed. The building I had been in was demolished and a fire had started at one end. Everything that had been so beautiful before was now grey and shattered. There were no people anywhere I could see, just uprooted trees, broken benches and rubbish. I could not recognise anything as I started to run. I only hesitated at the edge of the grass we were never allowed to step on and made the decision then to run straight over the grass in the direction of the tram terminal. All I could think of was get to my Mother in the city. I cried out loud "Mummy, Mummy" as I ran as fast as my small feet would take me.

When I got to the tram terminal, a tram was standing there forlorn, empty, smoke rising from it upwards in curls. All the windows were gone, the door gaped on its hinges and I realised I would have to run to my Mother's apartment in Tallinn, this tram was not going any place.

It was a journey I shall never forget. I could not recognise any landmarks, everything was different. The street was full of rubbish, stones, wooden blanks, trees, branches, shattered glass, holes in the footpath, roofs of houses leaning against each other or, blown away and I could see into the rooms like they were doll houses without walls. I saw people lying amongst the rubble on the street, unmoving, some I had to jump over, others I went around. It felt like I was the only person alive, there was nobody to help me. Acrid smoke was making my eyes smart and breathing hard, it was so dark even though it was still day time. I could hardly see as tears streamed down my face. The only light showing my way came from burning houses. I think it was mainly instinct that got me to my Mother's apartment in the end because I could not recognise any land marks at all. I ran up the stairs calling, "Mummy, Mummy".

The door was locked, she was not here. I sat sobbing onto the stairs and fell asleep. It was all a bad nightmare as I felt myself being wrapped into a silky, soft blanket and carried into bed. I could not open my eyes but felt warm hands caress my head and my Mother murmuring, "Sleep, baby sleep everything is well."

My Mother was at work when she heard the bombers overhead, there were so many of them and she knew this would be an all-out attack on Tallinn. She grabbed her coat and started running towards Kadriorg to get me out of the Kinder when the first bomb exploded nearby. A piece of shrapnel hit her between the eyes on top of her nose and she could feel the blood running down her face. Her eyes were affected and she could no longer see anything. Someone took her arm and led her to a bomb shelter where her wound was attended to. Luckily her eyes were not damaged and after a while her sight returned. The Wardens at the shelter stopped her from leaving until the all clear sounded and she was able to run to Kadriorg and back to find me asleep on top of the stairs. We moved to Merikula to my Grandmother's farm after this. Everything was normal there and life continued as before but it was not the same. The experience in Tallinn left us all shaken, very insecure and apprehensive of what was to come.

On Board Ship from Tallinn to Danzig

I awoke to loud voices from Grandmother's kitchen in Merikula.
My Mother and Grandmother were shouting at each other. I
quickly got dressed, took my doll and opened the door. My
Grandmother was standing near the stove holding my sister in
front of her and shouting at my Mother that she would rather die
than let my sister go to Germany to starve adding, what kind of
a mother was she to take her children into a war zone. I was so
glad to hear that I was included. My Mother retorted that the war
zone was here and she was going to save us all, Grandmother
included. Grandmother replied,

"You need to kill me first before I let Jungle go."

She had taken care of my sister ever since she was born.
Jungle was a breech baby and my mother nearly died giving birth
to her so Grandmother took over and tended to both until my
Mother was able to go to work again and Jungle was mostly reared
by Grandmother. Naturally they bonded and Grandmother felt
very close to my sister, more than to me.

My Mother saw me standing at the doorway and told me to
get my coat and boots, she said. "We are going." I was ready to go.

My Mother and I left the house to a large army truck waiting
outside Grandmother's door. The door of the truck's cabin
opened and my Mother lifted me into the cabin following me
into the seat. Uncle Wozniak was driving. He was my Mother's
friend, a German soldier, always helpful, happy and made me
laugh a lot. I felt secure driving with him through the pitch dark

night with no headlights. We stopped at the pier where a large ship was waiting. Uncle Wozniak carried me up the gangplank into the ship. The sailor at the top indicated that the ship was full, only place was on deck next to the toilet door. We made our way there and found just enough room for us to sit down. A lot of people were on deck already. It was dark but we could make out their shadows against the sky. Uncle Wozniak left and we made the best of where we were. This was an adventure even if a bit smelly sitting next to the toilet and I fell asleep leaning against the toilet door.

Imagine waking at daybreak to a sky beautifully coloured in a rosy hue and the ship far out at sea with no land visible. The world seems at peace, so quiet and serene until a sudden noise of an aeroplane makes everyone on deck sit up in visible panic, fearfully scanning the sky.

"Would the plane be friend or foe?"

. A huge plane appears overhead flying so low over the ship that you could just about touch it. It comes with guns blazing.

"Rattattatt, rattatatt, bullets spray the deck. Many people jump into the water, some stay inert on deck, others scream for help. The deck is quickly coloured bright red and rivulets of blood flow into the ocean.

The plane passes overhead so quick that you can hardly understand what happened. Then, high in the sky, you watch as the plane turns around and points its nose straight at you, coming for another run over the ship and this time it is aiming at you.

Your throat goes dry, your heart thumps furiously and you feel adrenaline shooting painfully into your stomach. You are in direct line of fire and have no time to think but so grateful for a quick thinking Mother who pushes you into the toilet and onto the floor laying her own body over you. You wish you could turn into a fly and crawl through the crack in the floor underneath as the bullets thud noisily against the toilet wall.

Then, the ship's anti-aircraft gun fires and it is comforting to hear as it joins in the ear deafening noise. The plane has another run over the ship and then it is quiet. No, not really because now you can hear the cries and screams of the injured and the shouts for help from the heads in the water.

My mother stands up from top of me and opens the toilet door to a horrifying picture with dead bodies everywhere. I can see some injured on deck alive, only the people who jumped into water, my Mother and I survived uninjured. I remember my body shaking involuntarily with fright, my throat so tight that not a sound comes out as sailors ran onto the deck to help people from the water. I could not stop shaking. One of the sailors carried me below deck into the ship where I was given warm milk and looked after until we docked in Danzig and my body stops shaking at last. My Mother stays on deck to help the wounded.

Danzig was a different world. I could not believe what I saw. It was like there was no war, like we had just had a bad nightmare on ship. Music was blaring from loudspeakers on street corners. People were laughing and dancing. Cafés were full of people even sitting out on the footbath eating, drinking and being merry. Soldiers marched and sang happy marching tunes. Everyone was so happy I could not believe it, had we just dreamt the massacre on board ship?

My Mother got a job in Danzig and life was good for a while. I became familiar with all the tunes of operettas and cabaret songs popular at the time as Mother not having a baby sitter for me, left me sitting in the park all day while she went to work. I have no idea what work she did but I was quite happy sitting in the park all day. There I met close up all the famous singers and stars of the era as they performed free for the people in the parks daily. Stars like Marika Rokk, Hans Albert, Marlene Dietrich. I cannot remember them all but life was wonderful, happy and carefree full of music and laughter. I can still remember the tunes but not the words to many classical pieces of music. I went to different parks during the day until I met Mother back from work at night. We rented a room and ate in cafes and life was good.

One incident brought back the nightmare on board ship when having coffee with my Mother in an outside Café one day. One of my Mother's close friends from Estonia passed by. My Mother called out to her and they were both overjoyed to meet. My Mother asked her about her daughter, Helga and her friend's face changed. They had also embarked on a ship from Tallinn, that ship had also been bombed by an enemy aircraft and their ship was sunk. She and her daughter found themselves in water clinging to a small piece of wood. They were in water for a long time and their hands were getting numb. The water was very cold, her daughter said she could not hold onto the wood any longer so her mother put her arms around her and treaded water, the piece of wood floated away and her daughter slipped from between her numb arms and sank into the deep sea right in front of her eyes. She went after her and lost consciousness waking on board another ship that had been nearby, rescuing survivors. She had been searching for her daughter Helga ever since, in the hope that she had also been rescued.

All of a sudden she stood up from the table with a funny look on her face, looking this way and that way shouting, "Where are you Helga, where are you, you naughty girl always running away." She then hurried away without another word and we never saw her again. A woman's body was picked up next day from the water nearby from where we had been sitting.

Danzig was our first stop in Germany and we always intended to travel on. One day there was no more music in Danzig. The city became quiet as the rumble from the front increased in the distance. More soldiers were hurrying along the streets but no more marching songs. Lorries full of soldiers, jeeps full of officers, finally tanks and cannon appeared in the street and people hurried into houses. Café's and shops boarded up their windows and parks became quiet and empty. The noise from the front became louder and we awoke one morning to a loud explosion. "Katushka" they called the Russian rocket thrower.

My Mother decided it was time to leave Danzig. Many others had the same idea as we crowded into the busy railway station. Some people had already slept there for days waiting for a train that never came or the ones that did, never stopped. We placed a blanket on the concrete floor and decided to wait also. Many trains came and passed full of soldiers and did not stop. The station became fuller by the day. We had been there already for two days when someone shouted, "Next train to Munich will stop here in 5 minutes."

Everyone surged to the front of the station and being so small, I was pinned between a lot of legs and felt nauseous. I needed air urgently so I started punching at the legs and made myself a passage out from between the legs, out of the station into fresh air and then promptly blacked out. When I came to, the station was no longer there. The rubble was half covering me and my mother. Luckily, when she saw me running for the exit she followed me and we escaped "Katushkas" deadly fire by seconds. The station received a direct hit and most of the people died there.

We were lucky, the heavy door into the station fell sideways and we were showered by glass but not the heavy timber which would have surely killed us had it fallen on us. Is it any wonder I believe in angels because they were surely watching over us on that day as we escaped only with a few scratches and I with a colossal headache which was to last for days and someone thought it might be concussion.

The front was getting nearer by the day and Mother decided it was time to start walking and we joined many others walking out of Danzig. I felt very queer, as though walking in a cloud and everything seemed in slow motion. My hearing was muted and I did not see well. Everything seemed like a dream and I did not seem to be quite present.

Uncle Wozniak appeared again from somewhere and when he bent down to look at me, it seemed like he was in a fish bowl or maybe I was in it. Uncle Wozniak would take us to the next town and vanish for a while, then come and take us in his army truck to the next location and so on. He took supplies to Staff and Generals in the army and had the opportunity to transport us as well. We also walked a lot and sometimes slept in ruins or haystacks, sometimes in people's houses. It was all like a dream and I do not remember exactly how we got to Vienna. The only one clear image from this long trek was one that impressed itself deeply into my mind and I still see it clearly even though decades have passed.

One day, on one of our stops, I was watching some boys play amongst the ruins of a house up the hill. They were throwing what looked like a funny shaped ball to each other and one of the boys caught my attention because he was as beautiful as one of my dolls I had back home. Golden blonde locks framed a rosy, round face with bright blue, very large blue eyes and I could not take my eyes off him. After watching the boys play for a while, my Mother called me and it seemed to be urgent. I turned and walked down the small hillside when suddenly the earth shook under me and I fell down.

A mighty explosion behind me made my Mother run to help me up and we hurried to where the boys had been playing as did

Rita Reet Danko

many other mothers. It turned out the boys were throwing a live grenade and it went off causing much damage. The first image I saw was the blonde, blue eyed boy. He was lying on the ground inert, blood bursting from his armpit. Something looked strange to me and then I saw it – his arm was lying far away from him all mangled and bloody. His blue eyes were huge, looking up to the sky unmoving. I then remembered pulling my doll's arms off so I could dress it easier.

We moved on the next day but I often wondered whatever became of that beautiful, doll like boy without arms because it could have been me had I stayed longer.

Vienna, Austria

Uncle Wozniak dropped us off in Vienna at Hutteldorf, Bujatigasse 17, Vienna. The house, a mansion really belonged to an old Baroness who lived in this huge house all alone. Vienna was full of refugees and there were no camps to accommodate all of us but there were a lot of large houses with men gone to war, people living in large houses with few occupants were required to give shelter to the refugees. The Baroness was pretty old and was not pleased to have to provide a room for us but she seemed to warm to me after a while. We were given the servant's quarter – one room and a small kitchen. A huge forested garden belonged to the house and I found it an ideal playground, spending lots of time there. To get to our room we had to cross the Baroness's lounge. This was of great interest to me, soft Persian carpet underfoot, large piano she never played, huge paintings covering all wall space and so many vases, sculptures and statues of all kinds. A musty smell hung over everything and I would have loved to inspect all the treasures closer but I was not allowed to linger or, heaven forbid touch anything. Each time we crossed the lounge the Baroness appeared in a doorway, sometimes I could just see her peeking through the crack in the door. She never talked and always seemed sullen or angry. It was quite uncomfortable crossing the lounge room but there was no way of avoiding it.

Bathroom, open toilet and the potato cellar were all in a small lean- to house outside as was the custom then. The house had another storey, the upper level which was commandeered by

German Officers. Knowing they were there made us feel quite secure.

Uncle Wozniak came often to visit, always bringing something good to eat. He came with his mouth harmonica and played happy dance music. He taught me rhythm by placing my bare feet onto his and then waltzing with me all around the Baronesses lounge room. The Baroness even looked happy on these occasions and did not mind us using her lounge room. Uncle Woznia made us laugh telling stories of his youth in Berlin when he went dancing with white "gemashen" over his shoes, the very height of fashion at the time. These were a kind of white leather overlay on shoes with black buttons on the side and very fashionable.

I remember the soft grey woollen blankets and a huge parachute made from real silk he brought. I remember those especially as later my mother made coats from the blankets and blouses from the parachute which we took to the country to barter for food when shops were empty and we were hungry for what seemed a very long time, but for the time being it was peaceful and I started Primary School. My Mother got a job as tram driver. She knew nothing about trams but women had to learn all kinds of jobs that were hereto only for men and they had to learn quickly. All able bodied men, except the very old and frail or young boys were at the front. Later even they vanished from the street.

Primary School did not last long as I kept fainting in class. The school doctor came and diagnosed malnutrition for which he wrote a prescription for milk coupons. The teachers did not want me disrupting the class by fainting and excused me from school. I rode trams with my Mother every day instead.

One day a loud siren sounded as we rode the tram. It was a sound full of danger and meant enemy aircraft approaching. The tram stopped and all the passengers ran to the nearest bomb shelter which was a huge concrete building that looked like nothing could ever destroy it. A soldier at the door beckoned us to quickly come inside as the bombers were already visible in the sky. He called out that this was one of the most secure bomb shelters in Vienna and we would be quite safe inside, deep down underneath the concrete floors.

I was already running towards the building when my mother suddenly pulled me away changing direction past the building, pulling me along up the street. I remember being quite upset because I could hear, then see the enemy aircraft in the sky and looking up I could see black oblong objects with fins falling from the belly of the aircrafts towards us in exact formation. I knew these were bombs and we were right underneath. The door of the huge concrete building was now closed and I panicked, we had nowhere to go, we were out in the open and in danger. I learnt early on that it was not the bombs that were as dangerous as the shrapnel that flew from them like missiles in every direction, maiming, injuring and killing people and any kind of shelter became imperative.

The first explosion shook the earth under my feet and my mother pulled me into the nearest doorway, a flimsy two storey wooden house that looked like it would topple over with a strong breeze. A security guard ushered us down the stairs into the cellar where lots of people were sitting along the walls. It was just the utility cellar for the occupants of the house who were all French Refugees. The cellar was only half way underground with the window on street level. The earth shook again and again, the small broken window was covered with a cloth and we could see the flashes of light and hear the earth shattering noise with each explosion. I thought we would all be dead for sure.

Our refuge seemed so insecure compared with the concrete building we passed by and I was still upset with my mother. The window lit up with each deafening, earth shaking explosion and the house was constantly shaking. People sitting there along the walls were praying, some were crying, all talking in a strange language. An old man kept reassuring everyone in German, that if it was God's will we would be OK. Then the staircase came toppling down and the single light bulb in the cellar went out and we were in pitch dark except for the flashes of explosions from the window. Then, the house trembled and shook, something fell outside the window and blocked even that light and plaster started falling from the cellar ceiling. We all moved into one corner and huddled together as part of the ceiling gave in. Breathing became hard as a lot of dust fell also. Mother gave me a handkerchief to hold in front of my eyes and nose and told me to breathe shallow.

Suddenly I felt something creep up my bare legs and I screamed with fright. The old man had a torch and as he switched it on, I saw to my horror ugly black water slowly creeping up higher and higher up my bare legs. The cellar was slowly filling up with water and I was terrified and so was everyone else. The people all talked louder and quicker.

Panic gripped my throat, an unbelievable urge to run, but to run where? We were closed in without escape. My Mother put her arms around me and calmed me down.

"We are all in the same boat and there must be something we can think of, if everyone stayed calm." She said.

The old man shone the torch around the ceiling as another piece of it fell and exposed a large black hole. My Mother said, "We will drown if we stay here" and lifted me up onto her shoulders pushing me towards the rim of that black hole. A young woman pushed my Mother aside and climbing on top of some rubble was able to lift herself up and crawl into the hole in front of us. Now everyone wanted to climb into the hole and people pushed, shoved each other yelling and fighting. It was terrible.

The house gave another huge tremble and the old man switched off his torch yelling at everyone to stop fighting.

"we can all escape if we stay calm.".

He switched the torch back on when everyone quietened down and helped my Mother push me through the hole telling me to crawl as fast as I can. My Mother followed me as I felt nails digging into my knees and glass cut my hands but I crawled until I could crawl no longer. The way was barred with something big and solid. Mother was directly behind me but the space was so small that she could only touch my feet and I could hear her. She told me to curl up, put the handkerchief over my face and go to sleep. She would think of something . I knew she would and curled up to go to sleep. At least there were no more explosions. The planes had dumped all their bombs over Vienna, done their job and left.

I don't know how long I slept, time had no importance. I woke to hear faint voices and called out. The voices stopped, so both Mother and I called together, this time as loud as we could. The voices came closer and louder. A breeze of fresh air swept suddenly over us from somewhere and then a most welcome sliver of day light high up above brought tears to my eyes. The sliver of day light became a hole big enough to frame a face asking if we were able to move our legs and arms.

Very soon strong arms lifted me out of my tiny prison and I could breathe fresh air. My legs were weak and wobbly so I sat down on a stone. Someone handed me a glass of water, it was the most welcoming, precious gift anyone could give me at that time. Mother and I just sat there and marvelled at being alive

Finally, I stood up and looked around, destruction surrounded me in every direction. Not a single building was standing as far as I could see. Everywhere was heaps of rubble and the street was unrecognisable. Fire could be seen in many places. Then, my mother was beside me and we held each other, not saying a word. I could feel warm tears of relief falling down my cheeks. We we survived.

We made our way laboriously over the ruins of a city towards where the concrete building should have been standing, but it was no longer there. Large slabs of stone and concrete covered the area and all the people in the shelter suffocated the falling concrete slabs buried them, we later heard. I felt so grateful then to my mother for not listening to me, instead running on and taking shelter in the little wooden house with the French refugees. Central Vienna was no longer standing. The beautiful historical architecture was completely destroyed and unrecognisable. It seemed so strange that even the street was gone. The horizon was empty. Where before there were large buildings, there was nothing now but heaps of rubble. The tram we had been in was crumpled up like a piece of paper, the ends of the track sticking up towards the sky. The air was eerily quiet, the bombers had left beautiful, historical Vienna in ruins and then, somewhere in the distance a church bell rang.

My mother took my hand and we walked. It was not easy as we had to climb over ruins and the rubble was still moving. I think we walked the whole night and I was so happy to finally see the Baronesses house, unscathed.

At last we were safe, or so we thought. That same night there was a thunder storm. The roll of thunder was as loud as the bombs and the lightning flashes were as bright as day light I was so scared, I crawled under the bed and covered my ears but I could still hear the noise and see the lightning flashes. My whole body was shaking with fright. My Mother said it was only thunder but to me it was like the bombs all over again. Eventually it stopped and I went to bed waking often with nervous spasms convulsing my whole body.

There were no more tram rides. There was no longer any order. Shops were looted and lawlessness ruled. We stayed inside the house and went to bed with our clothes on as sirens sounded often at night and we had very little time to make it to the cellar in the outhouse before the bombs started exploding. The Americans rained bombs on us during the day and the British came at night. After a while we became expert at picking which aircraft was in the sky as they had different sounds.

We had eaten all the food we had in the house and there was nothing left at all. I was so hungry that I felt my stomach gnawing at itself and sleeping was painful because I dreamt of eating so much bread that my stomach was full only to wake up with hunger pains. I did venture out to look into rubbish tins but they were empty as well. One day I came across a group of people slaughtering a dead horse in the middle of the street. I ran home to call my mother and bring a knife but by the time we returned there was only a red patch of blood left in the middle of the street. I was so disappointed and hungry that I stuffed my mouth full of leaves stripped from the nearest bush. Dogs and cats vanished from the streets and there were rumours that they were slaughtered and canned as beef. Everyone was hungry.

Hunger made my mother and I venture into the street to look for something to eat. One day, .we came across a crowd looting a cheese factory. Two women were fighting over a round of cheese. A nice large round of cheese was left on the side of the street as the women argued and retreated further away from the cheese. I nudged my Mother to go and pick up the cheese but she would not. Well, I was hungry so I went and casually rolled the round of cheese down the slight slope in the street to my mother without the women noticing it. Mother then picked it up and we ran. This was the only food we had for many days.

One night I awoke and saw my father bending over me. He

smiled as he tucked the blankets around my body. When he saw me awake he put his finger to his lips and said,

"shhh, .Go back to sleep, everything is going to be alright."

I remember being so happy knowing that everything would be alright now and went back to sleep feeling happily secure. In the morning my father was not there, I ran around looking everywhere but he was not there. I asked my mother,

"Where is Daddy?" She said "I don't know."

I knew this was the wrong question but I did not know how to ask the question for the right answer, so said nothing more. The air raid siren sounded again and we could hear the explosions in the distance at the same time. There was no time to run to the cellar so I crawled under the bed. I am still wondering if my Father was actually there or did I just dream it.

The ear shattering noise from the bombs continued for some time and most of Vienna was demolished. We lived in the outskirt so were saved from much physical damage but for the damage to our nerves, as the noise was deafening and we were continuously afraid. Eventually the bombs stopped and it was quiet for a while. We ventured out to look for food but there were no shops or markets, everyone was hungry. The Officers from the top floor left some bags of dried peas when they left and we nearly exploded eating boiled peas day in day out.

Occupation of Vienna

Bombs were replaced by gunfire which became louder and louder until one day Russian soldiers appeared on our door step with rifles pointing at us. My mother, speaking Russian told them that there were only us in this building and no one else. They pushed my mother against the wall and told her they would shoot her as she was a spy speaking Russian. Somehow my mother was able to convince them that she was no spy and after this episode she no longer spoke Russian.

The soldiers occupied the house and put up tents in the garden, got drunk, destroyed the Baroness's carpets by urinating on them, shot at the paintings and axed the piano. The Baroness, my Mother and I were shivering with fright in the little lean-to toilet cum bathroom and hoped they would not find us. Early in the morning when everything was quiet we ventured out and stealthily made our way to the nearest cinema building used as a refuge for women and children.

Many women and children were already there. The doors were guarded by three old German men who offered the only possible security for us as we lay down to sleep between cinema chairs. We stayed there for some time. One morning we heard that two Russian soldiers came to the door looking for women during the night. The old men told them there were really good women at the back, lead them out and killed them. This made us feel a little bit safer.

We stayed there until the Baroness insisted to go back home

urgently. When we got home we found the Russian soldiers still there; the officers occupying the house and soldiers making camp under the trees. We were told to go away this was now Russian territory. The Baroness sat down on the doorstep and started to cry. My mother asked if she could go and take her belongings and was told "no". Just then a cry went up from the soldiers making camp outside "SS, SS," they shouted. The officers ran out of the house and jumped into their jeeps, the soldiers got into trucks and they all left leaving everything behind, even the camp fire still burning. We could hear spurts of gun fire nearby and the house was ours again. We went in and locked the doors quickly. Later we heard that a group of Hitler youths surviving the fighting had banded together and decided to fight to the last man taking many Russians with them. SS was a specially trained Hitler army much feared by everyone.

We took the food left by the soldiers and proceeded to clean up the house. Luckily the soldiers did not return but made camp at a large government building nearby.

My Mother came home one day with a small baby in her arms. She said he was my brother. This was news to me and I wondered where he had been all this time. He was so tiny and cute, slept most of the time and no trouble at all. I was happy for him to stay.

At this time of my life TV and internet had not been invented, I had not heard of phones and very few people had radios. News and information came by word of mouth and we heard that the Russian soldiers were giving food to children at a certain camp. I went to investigate taking a milk-can with me just in case the rumour was true. I did find a camp where soldiers handed out cooked food to the children standing in a long queue which I promptly joined. Since I only had this one can, soup, veggies and bread was all ladled into it and I did not care, it was food to take home where we all shared it. Next day I took 2 milk cans and

I kept going every day for the only meal we all shared at home including the Baroness. She was now family.

One of the young soldiers paid special attention to me and always gave me extras. One day he said to meet him later and he would take me to where he lived and we would eat cake together. This sounded good to me and I went to meet him at the camp. We both left to walk to his place and I must have walked too slow as suddenly he picked me up and hoisted me onto his shoulders. This scared me a bit but I did not dare to say anything or struggle as I was afraid of falling. He turned into a stadium where a soccer match was in progress.

The stadium was full of drinking, noisy soldiers and I did not feel safe so I sat very close to my friend who put his arm around me and held me close to him. As the match progressed my friend got very excited and started stroking me where I felt uncomfortable and all of a sudden I had this urge to escape. I had this uncanny feeling of danger and I knew that I must get out of there. I told him I had to go to the toilet. He pulled me closer and said to wait the match will finish soon. I felt trapped until a goal was kicked and everyone stood up cheering, whistling and shouting. My friend jumped up on the bench to cheer and let go of me. This was my chance, I jumped on the bench also, only to jump down at the back and make my way out from between the shouting, whistling soldiers. I ran as fast as my small feet would take me, not looking behind and not stopping until I came to the toilet door. I stopped for a moment there to see if he was following but there was no one behind me so I kept running, out the gate and all the way home. Luckily my mother did not ask what happened because nothing really happened but I did not go for food the next day or the day after. I was scared but did not know why.

My mother decided then that she would go out looking for

food and I should stay and baby sit my baby brother. She found a black market doing good business at a certain location where people came to barter with soldiers, bringing their treasures for food. My mother had a lot of jewellery sewn into hems of our clothes for safe keeping which came handy now. Thanks to my father who gave her jewellery at every important occasion. One of his family members was a Jeweller and the whole family supported him by buying his work as gifts. One by one she bartered these for food until the last one which my father gave her to give to me when I was grown up. This was a ring with one beautifully grafted silver rose. My mother held it up and asked me to choose- the ring or food? This was not a choice really, I could not eat the ring so of course I chose food.

She went out and came back empty handed. Sadly a soldier took the ring and promised to bring her flour but he did not show up. Next day a truck showed up at our gate with a heap of flour on the back, he backed into the yard, tipped the tray and flour cascaded down into the yard, the soldier in the truck waved and drove off. We were left with a heap of flour taller than I in the middle of the yard. We brought out every container we could find to fill with flour. When we ran out of containers the Baroness brought out linen billow covers and we filled these also. My mother then invited the neighbours to come and take what they could, asking only in return for some bread if they baked it.

My mother used the flour packed into home-made paper cones to barter at the black market for jewellery and watches which she in turn bartered for food from the soldiers. Suddenly we lived quite well thanks to my father's gift and my mother's ingenuity.

One night uncle Wozniak appeared with two men in long black overcoats flanking him. He did not smile nor play his harmonica. He walked to my baby brother's cot, lifted him up and held him close, tears streaming down his face. He then kissed me, embraced my mother holding her for a long time and whispering in her ear, then left with the two tall men on either side of him. We never saw him again. Years later I asked my mother what did he say and she told me he was going to be shot. That was all she said and nothing more.

After the war finished, Vienna was occupied and split into four zones. American, English, French and Russian. We happened to be in the Russian zone and as an Estonian, my mother did not feel safe so when regrouping of people took place by the authorities, she said we were Germans but her papers said otherwise. All Austrian people living there were given food coupons. Everyone else was invited to join a camp (lager) where we would be fed, sorted and sent back to wherever we came from. My mother feared that if she went to a camp sorted by Russians, we would be sent to Siberia. She heard stories of some Estonians who went to those camps forcibly made to return to Estonia voluntarily and decided to give camps a wide berth.

We were hungry again. Now it was the Baroness's turn to feed us all but the coupon was only for one person and very meagre as such. My mother, never at a loss for inventiveness, borrowed the Baroness's sewing machine and made coats from the grey blankets that uncle Wozniak brought and blouses from the silk parachute. Trains were running again and some sort of order reigned, so we were able to take a train to the country and hopefully sell those clothes to country people for food.

We set out early one morning, mother and I carrying one coat and two blouses which took her two nights to sew. We got off the train at a small station with no houses nearby. We walked and walked until we came to a farm, then walked some more to the next until finally mother sold everything and we had sausages and a full tray of eggs. I picked some wild apples on the way back to the train and were very happy with our venture until we got off the train in Vienna. Lots of tall men in long black overcoats were waiting at the station. They cordoned off an area so that everyone coming from the train had to enter singly and everyone was searched.

My mother, carrying the tray of eggs was told to give them over as it was contraband. She could do nothing else but hold the tray out to him and just before he could take it, she tipped the tray and let go. A dozen eggs make a big splash falling onto concrete floor. The man was very angry and shouted at her grabbing her bag and pushing her aside. Somehow amongst all this we were able to silently slide away and get lost in the crowd. We still had the sausages as they were strapped to my body hiding underneath my coat. The eggs were smashed on the ground and all that man got was wild apples in the bag. This was a bad experience and obviously we had to find another way for food.

My Best Friend

Mother decided we had to leave the Russian zone and make it over the border to an American zone. She heard that people were well looked after there. She borrowed maps from the Baroness and after studying these for some time made her decision of where we would cross the border and leave Austria for Germany and American zone.

I was sorry to leave my friend, my only friend in Vienna. His name was Gunther and he lived over the bridge in Hutteldorf strasse. I met him while gathering chestnuts one day. Hutteldorf strasse was flanked by large chestnut trees and the fallen nuts were large and shiny and I loved to hold these smooth shiny nuts in my hand. Suddenly a voice behind me said "What do you do with these nuts?"

The boy behind me was a little taller than me but not much older and he said. "Come with me I show you what I do with them."

We walked to his house which was directly opposite the bridge joining Hutteldorf strasse to Bujatigasse where I lived. Chickens were running around his yard and it was pretty messy. Gunther lived there with his mother after his father was taken into the German army and did not return.

Gunther took me into a shed at the back where he showed me his collection of animals made from chestnuts. He used matches to stick the nuts together and asked me to bring him any used matches we had. I knew we had a full plate of them as gas lighters had not been invented yet. We spent many days together making animals from chestnuts and when winter came and it snowed, we went tobogganing together. Sometimes he pulled me, sometimes I pulled him on the toboggan and when we found a hill we sat on the toboggan together and used our legs to propel ourselves forward. We had lots of fun and I did not want to leave him. The day my mother said we were leaving, I remember holding Gunther around his waist with my two arms, burying my face on his chest and crying. He took my hands, held them and looked down into my face very seriously as he said.

"When I grow up I will find you even if you go to the end of earth."

This made me happy knowing that we will be together again, my very best friend and I. I ran home, skipping all the way. Next day we left.

Snow, Snow and more Snow

Early in the morning my mother strapped my brother into a rucksack for her back, took a suitcase in hand, gave me the bag with food, said goodbye to the Baroness and we set off on our journey. Several hours later we got off the bus at a picturesque small village with snowy mountains all around us. Mother took my hand and we started to walk up one of these mountains. We walked up and up, when we thought we had reached the top there appeared another mountain ahead, this kept repeating again and again, there seemed to be no end to it. I looked at my brother in the rucksack and was fascinated by the long icicle hanging from his nose. He was a good baby mostly sucking on the end of his blanket or sleeping. It was cold and I was very tired but my mother kept saying, "only a little bit further, only to the next mountain top."

There were many mountain tops to climb and we must have walked for hours, climbing endless, blinding, white, mountain tops. The sun suddenly vanished and a cold wind was blowing into our bodies, making it unbearably cold and difficult to walk. The landscape had changed as well, instead of soft snow the ground was now hard and icy. Crevasses appeared on one side of us that went deep down and looked like bottomless open, black mouths and for the first time ever that I saw my mother afraid.

She was now very vary of where we walked and poked her long umbrella into the ground, testing it before we walked. This made walking slow and cumbersome. Then suddenly it became dark. It seemed like the clouds descended and enveloped us in their misty, cold swirls of greyness, playing tricks on our vision by lifting and descending, forever moving. Eventually, Mother stopped, made a small wind break in the ground, laid down a blanket and said. "We cannot go any further."

She was afraid of falling into a crevasse as we could no longer see where we were going and decided to finish the day.

Ah sleep, sweet sleep. It was heavenly to lay down after walking all day. I was so tired that sleep overcame me quickly. It felt so good, I no longer felt cold and sleep was so sweet. I have never felt such a feeling of complete surrender until mother started shaking me and telling me to wake up. I did not want to wake up, sleep was so sweet but she did not stop shaking until I opened my eyes, quite annoyed because I did not want to ever wake up.

"Look up there, she said, can you see the shape of a triangle?"

She thought she saw the roof of a house through the ever moving dark clouds but wanted to be sure she was not hallucinating. I peered through the moving swirls of clouds and yes indeed, as the cloud lifted a bit, I also saw something that looked like the triangle of a roof. Mother quickly packed us up and we ran towards what happened to be a small hut not too far away.

The three men looked up in shock as we barged through the door. They could not believe their eyes that a woman with two small children had climbed the mountain. They jumped up and attended to my brother who was not moving any more. They massaged and rubbed him, one of the men got into a sleeping bag with him to warm his little body with his own. I was given a vile drink that burned my throat but as it hit my stomach a warm feeling went through my entire body and I went to sleep. The next day we were taken back down the mountain we had climbed so laboriously previously, now standing on back of the skis of two of the men, my brother in a rucksack again on the back of the third man.

Avalanches the previous day had made it impossible for us to go down the mountain to the other side and cross the border like my Mother intended. We were very lucky, the three men were Austrian mountain patrol and they only came up to the hut once a month regularly or if there had been an avalanche. They were very sympathetic to my mother's goal to cross the border and suggested another route. They suggested we take a bus in the village which would take us near another border crossing through the mountains to Germany but we should get off the bus one stop before as the last stop was heavily scrutinised by Russian soldiers and everyone was regularly checked.

We boarded the indicated bus in the village. My brother was in the rucksack again and just as we were ready to get off the bus before the last stop, two Russian soldiers carrying a dead deer stepped on. They laid the deer in front of the bus's exit and would not let anyone get off. One passenger, a young man jumped over the deer and off the bus, running into the night. One of the soldiers jumped off the bus after him. We heard a shot and the soldier came back into the bus laughing. Nobody dared to move after that. Everybody had to remain in the bus until the last stop. We were then all herded out by the two soldiers and marched to the border control check point. We all queued outside the hut, guarded by some soldiers.

My mother kept to the back of the queue as one by one the bus passengers were roughly pushed into the building. My mother handed me some papers and told me to make a hole in the snow and bury them pretending to build a snowman when the soldiers looked our way. I did as she asked me, burying our passports and all other identity papers.

The last passenger vanished into the building and we were left with two soldiers guarding us. After a while an officer came out of the door and lit a cigarette, then noticing us waved his hand and said "Go". He did not need to say this twice, we went as fast as our feet would allow without actually running. Maybe they had enough fun for the night or a mother with two small children did not look like she would attempt to flee over the border. Whatever the reason for letting us go without checking, we were happy they did.

It was dark when we crossed a small bridge and I suddenly found myself falling into soft snow. I had stepped off the bridge into snow that had built up over an icy creek and was as high as the side of the bridge. I was buried over my head in cold snow. My mother scraped enough snow away to free my head so I could breathe but she could not lift me out. She told me not to move and went for help to the nearest farm house. Two men came, each putting a hand under my arm pit and lifted me out of the hole. I was wet and shivered with cold as they carried me into the warm house, gave me a pair of pyjamas that were too big, a blanket to wrap around and invited me and my mother to join them for the evening meal. A large pot of thick hot broth was placed in the middle of the table, each of us was handed a spoon and a piece of bread and we all helped ourselves from the pot. Many people were already there, all waiting for a guide to take them over the border and we all ate from the same pot. This was funny for me but I was hungry, we had not eaten since this morning on top of the mountain with the patrol men.

My fall into snow was lucky as this bridge was exactly next to the house we were told by the mountain patrol men to look for. This farm house belonged to a "people smuggler" only then they were called guides and we considered ourselves lucky to find someone to take us over the border, especially after the mountain episode where we nearly died. After eating, we and all the others waiting there bedded down on the floor in the same room.

I was happy to be in that farm house for a few days as we were given breakfast and dinner and the house was warm. Someone gave me a fantastic treasure – a huge book containing all the Grimm Fairy Tales. I have never seen such a beautifully gold bound huge book. Every Fairy tale started with an embellished letter which was a work of art in itself. The book was illustrated with glossy colourful pictures and the cover had much gold decoration. When you closed the book all the pages created a soft sheet of gold on each end and on the side. It was the most magnificent gift and I treasured it greatly rereading every story again and again. In time my own children enjoyed the very same stories as I remembered them, "Hansel and Gretel, Snow White, The Frog Prince, The little Mermaid, The Golden Goose" and many more. I wept bitterly when I had to leave the book behind as it was too large and heavy to carry when we were eventually told we could go. I hope that many more refugee children waiting at the house enjoyed it. I still appreciate the memory of it and have never found anything like this magnificent book in my long life. I hope the next child inheriting the book appreciated it as much as I did.

The guide arrived but initially refused to take us. My brother was too small and if he cried then the whole group could be in danger. Somehow my mother convinced him to take us and swore that my little brother would not cry. Indeed, he did not as he slept most of the time in my mother's rucksack. Milk boiled with poppy seeds was a well- known relaxant and sleep inducer for children.

We silently moved out of the farm house one after another into the dark night. The darkness made the person in front of us just barely visible as we had to step into the foot prints of the person in front so that it looked like only one person walked in the snow. I was too small to be able to do this, so one of the men carried me. We moved like shadows between the forest trees, stopping every time there was some noise or a branch cracked underfoot. We stopped often and listened, only moving on when everything was quiet. There was no moon and it was so dark when snow started to fall. This was exactly the environment the guide was waiting for as no border guard in their right mind would venture out of their warm hut on a night like this.

Eventually we came to a river. This was a torrent gushing out of a mountain and rushing down the ravine like boiling water, spewing spray all around. Spanning this boiling cauldron was a wooden blank for us to cross. The blank was bent from layers of ice formed from the spray of water and moved from side to side like a swing.

They tied a rope around my middle and I was told to sit on this blank as they pulled me across this ever moving, icy blank. The skin on my hands was burning as I tried to hold onto the sides of the blank and my face was peppered with icy water spraying from below. I was told not to look down into the rushing water underneath me. It looked like an angry, roaring witch's pot.

This was the most frightening experience of my short life. I was sure glad to be pulled up from this icy blank on the other side, all wet, cold, with numb hands and hurting but grateful to have made it. We walked in the snow again, silently but this time not in the foot prints of the person in front. We had passed the border and were in no man's land but the danger of being shot by the border guards was still there.

In the distance we could see lights from houses and soon came upon a house where we were welcomed into a warm room, blankets and warm milk was provided. We had made it successfully out of Austria, the Russian zone and into Germany. Next day we boarded a train to Munich.

It was a very short train ride. The train came to a sudden halt and everybody was ordered out. We were herded into a place that used to be a Concentration Camp in Dachau and some people panicked but we were told not to fear as the war had ended, there was no more danger and we would only be sorted in this place and sent back home shortly. This was what my mother definitely did not want, to be sent back to Estonia and since we had no passports or papers she told them we were Sudeten German Refugees with no home to go back to.

Dachau

The camp had many large huts and rooms with triple bunk beds and only one pot belly stove in the middle of the room for warmth. It was very cold as this one little stove could not heat the whole room and we were not provided with enough wood or coal to feed it. We used the wooden blanks from under our mattresses to burn. I lost all the blanks from my bed except three as I was small and three blanks holding the straw mattress were deemed to be just enough for a small body.

One day as I warmed myself beside the stove a large fat louse dropped from my long hair onto my jumper. My mother ran to me as I screamed and more lice were dropping onto my jumper. My hair was full of these awful bugs. Mother borrowed a pair of scissors and cut all my hair off, dropping each strand into the fire. She then got some kerosene from somewhere and rubbed it into my head. This made my head itch terribly and also meant I could no longer warm myself near the stove as I might catch fire but soon I was happy to be free of those awful lice.

People came into this camp and went again, but we stayed on as my Mother's story of our nationality and where we came from could not be verified. We stayed on, often in an empty barrack with lots of empty beds and I had nothing to do. We did have the pot belly stove all to ourselves and we demolished a lot of blanks from unoccupied beds to keep warm. I had no toys, not even paper or pencil to draw on. I was bored and I had to occupy myself the best I could.

I amused myself by singing, I remembered a lot of tunes from Danzig's free music for the people in the park. They were mostly Viennese operettas and popular German Cabaret music of the time. I did not remember the words but the tunes came easy. I was encouraged to sing by my little brother as he would tap his feet and pirouette, inventing his own dance steps, laughing all the time. This was fun and I wished we had music. Then I remembered the man who played spoons in the park and I thought I could do it too.

The day I became a spoon thief the mess was full of people and it was easy to drop a spoon into my pocket at lunch time. At dinner another spoon dropped into my pocket and I had my percussion instrument. With a bit of practice we had rhythm to my voice and my little brother danced and laughed until he dropped. I loved playing the spoons, it gave me an interest and creative outlet as well as making my little brother happy. It was wonderful to see his cherubic face crinkle up with laughter as his skinny body swayed and turned to the rhythm of my spoons.

One night the ambulance came and took my little brother away. I heard them say it was his lungs, they collapsed, I actually saw the hole in his back, it was as large as my fist. I lost my little companion, my partner, my interest and my music, I never played the spoons again. I felt lost and sat around doing nothing all day, it was like losing part of myself. I desperately wanted him back.

We were told that he might die and needed an operation, this would cost money my mother did not have. She told them to go ahead, she would find the money somehow. In the meantime my mother found that there was an Estonian Consulate in Munich and she now told the Camp Administrators that we were actually Estonians, not Germans and she wanted them to send us to Munich. It would take some time for this new information to be verified but we could not go anywhere anyway as long as my brother was in hospital.

My mother went begging for money to pay the hospital but nobody had any and the Camp Administrators said no as well. One day a man and a woman came to see my mother and offered her money to pay for my brother's hospital but they wanted to keep my brother in return. They told her that it will be difficult for her alone with two small children and since they did not have any children themselves, they would gladly take my brother as their own and look after him better than she could.

I was so glad to hear mother say "no way would she sell any of her children and she would find the money somehow" I prayed she would but the lack of money remained.

When my brother was well again that same couple very kindly paid the hospital bill with no strings attached and without taking my brother in exchange. I was so glad to have him back. He was pale and even skinnier than he was before; his smile was feeble and he could not stand on his feet, no more dancing for a while. They said he needs good food and rest. The Camp provided food and we hoped it was good for him, he was not hungry and we had to coax him to eat. I stayed at his bed side and told him stories. Stories I remembered reading from that magnificent gold leaf book I had to leave behind in the farm house. Stories like Snow White, Jack and the Beanstalk, Hansel and Gretel, and a special story I made up about a small boy called Peeti who could fly.

My little brother loved to hear the story of Peeti. Peeti could pluck stars from the sky which became sugar coated biscuits in his hand and he flew to distant lands where bread rolls hung from tree branches, rivers ran with milk and his fingers would be sticky picking sultanas from bushes. He wanted to hear about Peeti again and again and sometimes he would even add to the story. I am sure he imagined he could be Peeti and fly. I told this story again and again until I was tired but he could not have enough of Peeti's adventures and he often went to sleep with it. This was his story, he was Peeti and he was able to fly for a little while and I could see he was free of pain for the time that Peeti flew. He slept a lot and I am sure he even dreamt of being Peeti.

We became very close my little brother and I. I was with him most of the day as there was nothing else to do. People came into the camp and went again, we were the only ones that stayed.

Then one day, the news came to pack and we were free to go to Munich and the Estonian Consulate would pay our train fare.

Munich, Germany

The train was crowded, we were in a compartment with lots of other people. My brother sat on my mother's lap and I on the small suitcase we had for change of underwear when my brother suddenly became ill again. A nurse came from somewhere and said my brother had measles. The people all left the compartment and my brother could lie down on the seat as there was so much room now. He was very hot and red in the face, a rash developed visibly on his little skinny body. He was unconscious and we took turns to wash his face and body with a cold wet rag dropping small drops of water between his lips.

It seemed forever for the train to reach Munich and when it did there was an ambulance waiting to take my brother to hospital. Mother and I made our way to the Estonian Consulate by tram.

The Consulate was a huge building with very few people and lots of empty rooms with empty beds. We could choose where to sleep. There was not much to do and I amused myself with painting and drawing. I had no paper or pencil but I found some red berries that were good squashed up and substituting for red paint, charcoal from the oven was my drawing implement, some feathers I found a bird had left behind for a brush and lots of clean concrete foot path to be creative on. I left the walls alone as I had been caught and punished before, drawing on the nice white kitchen wall in Estonia.

I missed my little brother and lack of food was always a

problem for us. Germany had been heavily bombed during the war and shops were empty, there was none or very little supply. Munich was in the American zone and they transported basics in by planes but there never seemed to be enough for everyone and I was always hungry. Since we were the only refugees occupying the Consulate, we did not qualify for a cook and my mother was told she would have to do the cooking and the Consulate supplied the raw ingredients. This created one big problem as my mother never learnt how to cook, grandmother did all the cooking at home and my mother went out to work. My mother was not even interested in cooking, she could sew but not cook. I remember we ate a lot of raw cabbage at the Consulate. Bread was rationed but never enough, at least there was some. I still dreamt that one day I could eat enough bread to be fully satisfied.

It seemed such a long time when we finally got word that we could pick up my brother from the hospital. Two nuns brought my brother out and I could hardly recognise him, he was chubby and his hair was long and fell around his angelic face in blond curls. He looked like a little doll, so pretty. He had a new coat and lovely red boots, I just wanted to run up and hug him but when he saw us coming towards him and realised we were there to take him away, he started screaming, stamped his feet and yelled "Ich will nicht." In German. Translated to "I don't want to." Threw himself onto the ground and kept yelling, kicking his new red boots into air.

The nuns quickly turned and vanished into the building and I had this suspicious thought that this was not my brother. They must have exchanged my placid, happy little brother to this yelling, bad tempered little boy they did not want. I looked at my mother and wondered what she would do? She promptly gave him a slap on the backside, yanked him up and told him to march. He was quiet now but looked so angry and sullen. He did not want to go into the tram and threw another tantrum and got another slap. All the people in the tram looked at us and I pretended I did not belong there.

At the Consulate, he did not want to eat, throwing the plate with special boiled eggs, a rare treat, onto the floor.

I could not understand this change and wished it would go away, this new child was most disturbing to me and I was afraid of his angry outbursts. I tried to avoid him as much as I could and spent more time drawing on the foot paths.

One day the Consulate asked for me and my mother to see him. He had complaints from the neighbouring people about my "dirtying" the surrounding foot paths and wanted me to clean it up. He said to my mother that I should be in school and promised to do something about it as soon as the foot paths were all cleaned up.

My mother helped me wash the foot paths as I cried. My art was not dirt on the foot path, I was so hurt and this was obviously the end of a graffiti artist and I was apprehensive of what would follow. I had not been to school since the bombing in Vienna and I was afraid. School sounded like a punishment for having too much fun painting the foot paths.

Deshingen - Ingolstatd

We were on the train bound for Ingolstadt, my mother, brother and the small suitcase with our change of underwear. My brother was still angry and sullen but there were no more outbursts. The change in him made me very sad and I missed my happy little brother who was a delight to have instead of this angry sullen little boy I was afraid of and who did not want to have anything to do with me or anyone else.

He was too small to understand but who could blame him for not wanting to return to poverty after being pampered and living well with the nuns. They provided him with everything he wished for and my Mother could not.

The train arrived in Ingolstadt and we got into a bus - destination, " Deshingen". A camp housing Estonian refugees that was originally built for the workers and their families of an oil installation nearby. The camp consisted of approximately 50 brick, twin, two storey buildings, divided by hedges, each with their own small garden and ready-made dug up garden beds for planting. We were allotted an attic apartment with 2 rooms, one of these also used as a kitchen. The rooms were sparsely furnished and fairly small but it was good to have a home. My mother was assigned work in a factory in nearby Ingolstadt; my brother to Kindergarten and I to School, both within the camp.

My first day in School was disastrous, I did not speak a word of Estonian, I had completely forgotten it. We had been speaking German ever since we left Estonia and I was too young then to have learnt it properly. Nobody spoke German in this School and I felt utterly alien. I also felt embarrassed, for the first time in my short life my attention was directed to the clothes I was wearing. I only had this one dress and I was rapidly growing out of it. The other girls looked and sniggered whispering and laughing. I can still feel their haughty looks on me. I sat on my own and did nothing. I could not wait for School to finish, I just wanted out of there.

The teachers must have also noticed my predicament. One elderly teacher caught my arm as I was leaving and suggested she walks me back to my quarters as she lived in the same house on the lower level. She invited me into her room and suggested she would teach me Estonian after School. She made me feel comfortable by showing me photos of her daughter who died in a bombing raid and wished she had too. This was something I could understand and sympathise with. She also spoke German with me making me feel at home.

When my mother arrived, she called her in and told her that a parcel had just arrived from a charity organisation in America and we might go and see if there was something there we could use. She took us to the Administration Building and into a room where a lady was sorting clothes. There were lots of open parcels on a table and she said to go and take what we wanted.

My mother selected a couple of dresses for me and also for herself and something for my brother and I got a new pair of shoes, mine were just about disintegrating on my feet I did not even realise that my toes were peeping out of my broken shoes. This was heaven, just to be able to go and take what I wanted was wonderful but also made me aware of the importance of clothes and that other people looked and compared and judged you by what you wore.

Every night after School I learnt Estonian, every day in School

I did nothing. Slowly, so very slowly I started to understand what was being said in School and life started to become somewhat normal. Food was still scarce, I was always hungry. The camp provided some basics for me lunch time at School but since mother was working now she was supposed to cook and take care of us. Mother still did not know how to cook.

I made some friends in Deshingen, Eva, Olga and Ulli. They were cousins and I stayed friends with them even after leaving the camp and emigrating. Summer came, then autumn and winter and spring again. I could understand and speak Estonian passably by now. I still went to see my private teacher every afternoon after school, she had become like a warm Grandmother to me and I loved to sit and listen to her stories. She loved to discuss politics, history and geography and I came to realise why wars had to be or not to be. She often had discussions with herself and I was the benefactor of her wide knowledge, wisdom of world affairs. We complimented each other well, she loved to talk and I to listen

Deshingen was beautiful in spring. I could not remember seeing so many apple blossoms in one place. Many of the Estonians there planted their garden beds with vegetables and I thought I might do the same. We were allotted a bed in the garden that no one had been using for some time and the earth was quite hard. I had no digging tools and used a sharp edged stone to loosen the earth for some tomato seeds I salvaged from the kitchen. Needless to say they came to nothing and I was so envious looking hungrily at everyone else's flourishing garden beds. Our neighbour's garden was lush with cucumbers and I have never tasted better cucumbers than the ones picked fresh, eaten still with earth on them from our neighbour's garden.

My mother loved to go dancing on weekends to Ingolstadt and she had no one to go with. Since I was developing rapidly, she recruited me to go with her and I loved it. Men were scarce after the war and mostly women partnered each other at those dances. I learned a lot of different dance steps dancing with different women and loved to move my body to different rhythms, remembering my little brother's body movements as he danced to my spoons I think I did quite well. I also started to take note of what the women were wearing, their hairdos, shoes, jewellery and grooming. It was satisfying even to just sit and observe. I was growing up. Then, my mother had a friend, a male friend to go dancing with and I was sadly left at home.

One day, everyone in the camp was called to a meeting in the big hall and we were told that we could not stay in this camp forever and needed to think of our future. As war refugees from Estonia we were entitled to immigrate to another country for free and several countries offered refuge. My mother made an application to Australia and the USA and she said she would go to whichever country answered her application first. To everyone's surprise it was Australia. Surprise because Australia had a reputation of taking single men and women not women with children.

Good Bye Europe

We were packing again, going to another camp somewhere in Germany. There had been a few, they were called transfer camps. They came with a bus or lorry, called your names and you slept in another bed again. There were interviews, doctor's checks, ID photos and paper work. Last camp was in Hamburg and we were there for a longer time waiting for the next ship to come and take us.

My mother was assigned to kitchen duty. She did not want to go to, so I went instead. I wanted to learn to cook as I thought that then I might never be hungry again. Alas, it was peeling potatoes I learnt. Together with many other women I was given a small knife, a chair to sit on and a large bag of potatoes. The woman next to me showed me how to peel a potato and selected the smaller ones for me as my hand was too little to even hold most potatoes. She kept instructing me to make the peel thinner and not waste the potato. I wondered why we peeled at all as we boiled potatoes in Vienna with their peel on and this seemed to me less wasteful of the potato but I did as I was told.

I learnt to peel and love it. Not the peeling part as I never satisfied the woman next to me as to the thinness of the peel but I loved to listen to the stories the women told, especially the cooking stories and I learnt the finer points of cuisine before I even held a ladle in my hand. I encouraged the women to talk by asking questions and they all loved to talk about food, most likely they were as hungry as I was. Potatoes could be done in so many ways, fried, baked mashed, chipped, grated, added to soups, fried with onions, made into bread, pancakes, rissoles, even cakes. Ah, the cakes some of these women could make made your mouth water. I made the resolve there and then that I was going to be the best cook ever when I grow up. I imagined that being able to cook, there would always be food and I would not be hungry.

My potato peeling days came to an end eventually when we were told that a ship called Anna Salen, bound for Australia was ready and waiting for us. The name of this ship was like a good omen as my Grandmother's name was Anna Salemaa, so very similar. This ship used to be an aircraft carrier during the war, quickly converted into carrying refugees after the war and we were going to Australia in it. All I knew about Australia was that it was very hot there, so hot that if you dropped an egg onto the pavement, it fried within seconds.

An army lorry came to take us and others to this ship, it looked huge and it was going to be our home for the next six weeks or so. Good bye Europe as we walked up the wooden gangplank and up to our ship.

We stood along the railing with everyone else as the ship slowly left the wharf at Bremen Hafen. Some people cried but I was glad to be leaving all the bad memories behind. I was too young to know that no memories are ever left behind, we carry all of them with us to the very end.

Men and women were separated and we were taken down a narrow winding staircase to a room with lots of double bunks tightly spaced together and no other furniture. We had no trouble finding space for our small suitcase on the bed. I always got the top bunk, no exception this time. Mother and my brother were below me. There were no windows and the air was not good but we were told this place was for sleeping only, day time we would be up on the deck. The room filled up with women, my neighbour was a young woman who cried a lot. She never spoke a word just sobbed and this made me very sad. I wished I could say something but I did not know what so I pulled the blanket over my head and went to sleep.

We were given paper bags for sea sickness and told to drink lots of water. The ocean was calm for many days until one night the ship started swaying from side to side. Gently at first, but then more and more forcefully. Some women started moaning, others were crying, then some vomited. I knew why we were given those paper bags. The stench in the cabin became worse and worse and my Mother decided we were not going to be sick from it and took me and my brother out of our beds, got us dressed and we left the cabin.

As we climbed the stairs upwards an officer barred our way, telling us that it was too dangerous to go on deck and would we please get back to our cabin. My Mother pleaded to be allowed to have some fresh air as the cabin was intolerable and we did not want to be sick from the smell down there. She said she would do anything to be able to escape the foul air in the cabin. The officer asked if she would work. My Mother repeated, she would do anything and that is how we became "Bucket Chuckers."

The officer said he would look after my brother and teach him to play chess, he needed someone to play with whom he could beat at the game while Mother and I would carry the buckets of vomit from below up the deck and throw the contents overboard. I thought that maybe it was easier to be sick like everyone else but Mother had already made up her mind she would rather be a Bucket Chucker and sleep strapped to a deckchair in the fresh air than sleep with the moaning women and the smell below. I had no say in this, it was decided.

It took a few spilt buckets before we got expert at juggling the moving stairs and rolling deck. We needed to synchronise since

I was so much smaller than my Mother, each holding one end of the bucket then heaving the content overboard. Only once were we sick and that was when we threw the content up wind instead of down and collected the whole stinking bucket on ourselves. We carried those buckets as long as the women were sick down stairs and learnt to stay on our feet as the deck heaved from one side to another. Waves of salty water washed over us, which was good as it cleaned up whatever we spilt. I only fell once and slid all the way to the railing, holding onto it for dear life. Mother told me never to let go of the bucket if I fell as the bucket would stop me going over the rail.

This was dangerous work as the deck was slippery from the waves washing over it and the constant spray peppering our faces made us temporarily blind but there were advantages doing this work, we were treated like crew, free to go where others were not and we got our own private sleeping cabin. Often we were the only ones eating in the mess and had as many extras as we wanted. The cooks were all Italian and I became quite fond of spaghetti. When the storm was blowing a hurricane, we could not hold onto the plates as they slid from one end of the long mess table to the other. My brother and I would then sit at each end of the table and take a quick spoonful as the plate whizzed towards us before it slid to the other end again and so forth. This made eating fun and at last I was no longer hungry as there was plenty to eat.

When the weather eased and there were no more buckets to chuck, Mother and I found other work, like doing washing for the officers. I learnt how to use a wash board. This was just a piece of corrugated iron surrounded by a wooden frame and you rubbed the soaped clothe up and down on it and even my small hands could do that. I was so busy that I did not even know that I had my thirteenth birthday on board ship until we crossed the equator and was told that thirteen was too young to be christened by King Neptune. Not that I wanted to as I watched women and girls being carried to the pool and thrown in. Men jumped in themselves. Watching this from the upper deck I was very glad I was thirteen and escaped this silly tradition.

Australia & Bonegilla

It was July 1950 when someone shouted "Land ahead." We all ran to the railing to see and were told then to keep back as we could capsize the ship. There was a debate going on about the land we saw as being Australia or not. Australia was supposed to be a hot country and since we were shivering with cold, it could not be Australia. It was a very cold July Melbourne morning.

We berthed at Port Melbourne Pier and the ship's Bursar called Mother and me into his office. We were going to be paid for the work we had done on board. I think even Mother was surprised and I even more when after paying her, the Bursar called my name, asked me to sign a paper and handed me some money. My very first pay ever. I cannot remember how much it was but it certainly was a most pleasant surprise.

We packed our one suitcase and left to be taken to a waiting train bound for Bonegilla, another transfer camp. On the pier was a small shop and in the shop window I saw a huge block of chocolate, a half- pound block of Cadbury milk chocolate. I vaguely remembered what chocolate was like but that was an eternity ago. I asked my Mother if I could use some of my wages to buy this chocolate, she said yes and kept walking to the waiting train.

My English was limited and I had no idea how to ask for the chocolate, so decided to just point and say "how much?" We had some English lessons on board ship and we learnt that Australia had pounds, shillings, pennies and half pennies as their monetary system at the time. The lady behind the counter said something like two an -sixpence -hapny. I knew what two and sixpence was but what is hapny? The lady saw my confusion and said "show me the money you have?' I placed all my money on the counter and she took some of the money and gave some back to me together with this huge block of chocolate.

It was the most exciting moment in my life. My first wage and my first purchase in my new country. I proudly held the half pound Cadbury chocolate as I walked to the train when a group of young boys espied the chocolate in my hand. They started to surround me and demand I give them the chocolate. I was certainly not going to do that and sprinted past them. They got to the door of the train wagon first and stopped me from going in. I saw my Mother sitting there talking to someone and called

"Mummy, catch."

Throwing the chocolate towards her at the same time. Before she realised what was happening, the chocolate hit her in the eye.

The boys ran away as quickly as they could, leaving me standing there aghast, watching my Mother holding her eye and screaming at me. Someone called the doctor, who came and attended to my Mother's eye which swelled up very fast and closed. She was so angry she slapped my face very hard and did not speak to me the entire journey to Bonegilla. My sincere utterance of how sorry I was did not help and on top of it all I never found the chocolate and have no idea what happened to it.

The rest of the trip was an unhappy event. Mother holding the ice to her eye which started to change to a very ugly colour and I tried to make myself as invisible as I could.

The train finally came to a stop and we were transferred from the train to camp, Bonegilla. This used to be an army camp and we stood in line for the usual routine to register, then doctor's check-up and another queue to receive a shirt, skirt, underwear and shoes, blankets and a pillow, then another queue where we received a plate, cup, spoon, fork and knife each. Everywhere my Mother was asked about her eye. She told them she ran into a door while she looked at me with her good eye like she was going to murder me. The eye really looked bad and the doctor referred her to the clinic where they put a patch on her eye and then it did not look that bad anymore and people stopped asking questions.

We were billeted in a large hut with many other women. Everyone had a bed and nothing else. In the morning someone beat a gong and we were told this was for breakfast. We took our plate, cup and cutlery and left the hut. Walking under some trees we were suddenly attacked by angry birds. One woman had her head cut open and was bleeding, the rest of us all put our plates on our head and ran. This was unexpected and like running a gauntlet, these birds were really dangerous, we had never experienced anything like this and avoided going under trees afterwards. We heard of poisonous snakes and spiders in Australia but did not expect dangerous birds.

We arrived at the mess hall. Long trestle tables were stretched out across the room but what made my eyes pop was that on every table, a foot or so apart were piles of bread and jam and butter and marmalade and more bread. I was in heaven, my wish was fulfilled. I could eat as much bread as I wanted and then some more. What bliss .On top of this there was warm cooked food, I cannot remember what but I always went back for seconds and whatever my brother left I finished as well. Of course this started to show very soon as I put on a lot of weight but I could not stop eating.

I learnt to swim in Bonegilla. There was an artificial lake nearby with trees growing in it and when the weather became warmer most youngsters found their way there. Bonegilla had no fences around the camp and we could go wherever we wanted but there was nowhere to go and we had no maps. We were well taken care of in the camp, why leave. We were told the water was treacherous with many springs and underwater currents but nobody was deterred, we still went. I could not swim and said this to someone. They promptly pushed me into the water and I paddled for dear life while everyone laughed because the water was shallow enough for me to stand up and walk. I watched those that could swim and copied them but I did not like to put my head under water and still don't even though I can hold myself on top of the water now and even float on my back.

We stayed in Bonegilla longer than most as my Mother was difficult to place for work. She still could not cook and women were mostly placed into service as housekeepers. Eventually we were found a place in Benalla where there was a shirt factory and Mother was happy to leave Bonegilla. We were taken by bus to camp Benalla. The camp in Benalla was next to an air field and used by air personnel during the war and about a kilometre out of the town. It now housed displaced people from all over Europe like us.

Mother went to work at the shirt factory called "Latoof and Cahill" in Benalla I went to school and my brother to Kindergarten. I could not speak much English and school was difficult for me as well as the teachers. They did not know what to do with me as remedial English was not invented yet and no one could help me. Eventually I did pick up enough to pass at school but I felt very much an outsider.

My Mother could not afford to pay for the school uniform so she bought some material and made it herself. It looked like the others but did not fit and I was often asked what was wrong with my uniform. She could only buy some books for me and I had to borrow the rest from other students. What I most missed was a red lead that everyone in school had except me. We were asked to underline with red and use it extensively in our exercise books. I really felt inferior not having a red pencil like everyone else. I heard the teachers say, "Why can't they be like all the others." Meaning, all the children from the camp were different and many of us did not have enough money to buy what we needed at school as women were paid much less than men, nor did we speak the language. The teachers did not seem to have an inkling of what it was like not to have enough money and feeling inferior because we were different from the others and they did not know what to do with us either.

It was a hot dry summer and it looked like everyone from the school went to the milk bar at recess to buy an icy pole except me. The other girls asked why I did not have an icy pole and I could not say that I lacked the penny needed to buy one so I just shrugged and left. All I really wanted was this one penny for an icy pole. Learning to speak English was hard as no teachers were assigned to us for this purpose. I could not do my homework as I did not understand what was required or I got it wrong. I think the teachers just passed me as they did not know what else to do with me .They had not been prepared for teaching us foreigners and were as much confused as we were. It was a matter of swim or sink and somehow the human mind always finds a way to swim.

Time passes, I learnt English and I grew up. We moved to Melbourne. Mother got a job in a geriatric hospital at Parkville. I was going for a job interview to an Assurance Company and we went shopping for a new outfit for me. Skirts were down to the ankles at the time and we bought a dark blue skirt with a fold at the back. A short fitted jacket matched the skirt. The hat I selected was small, white with a short veil that just covered my eyes. Short white gloves, black high heeled patented shoes and a black leather bag finished the outfit. My Mother always said, "Nobody sees what you eat but everybody notices what you wear." I was certainly looking my best for the job interview and it felt good to look like everyone else.

I stepped out of the Colonial Mutual Life Assurance Society's office in Collins Street where I had just clinched my first job on my first interview and stood at the corner of Collins and Elizabeth Street in Melbourne Australia in my new outfit feeling on top of the world. It was 1954 and my world was full of promise.

I was seventeen and the angels had been good to me.

Epilogue

My Mother lived to the age of 85, working at the Royal Melbourne Hospital for most of her life as a nursing aide. She loved her work and I am sure her "Never give up" attitude helped many of her patients.

My little brother is now a healthy seventy year old, married to the lovely Carol in Sydney.

I have a Hungarian husband whose background is similar to mine. He escaped Hungary during the 1956 revolution, arriving in Australia in 1957. We have four children and three grandchildren.

When I started writing this book, I am sure my Mother's Spirit woke me every morning at 3 o'clock without fail and compelled me to get out of bed to write another segment. Thus, unwillingly I relived my childhood every morning, remembering small segments at a time. I tried to write the memories as a child without an adult's view point but I am not sure whether I was always successful.

This book is foremost a record of our background for our children to know as how and why we came to Australia but I am hoping that others will also learn what it is like to live in the middle of war especially as a child. Not every child was as lucky as I, many did not make it out alive. My wish is that someone, somewhere will make my book into a film so that more people will see it and perhaps have some influence in stopping the suffering and destruction a war creates.

Reet Danko
Ballarat 2016

My Father, I, my Sister and Mother in Kadriorg, Estonia.

My Grandfather Raavel, my Father Viktor, uncle Johannes,

uncle Willhelm and Grandmother Rosalia In Tallinn, Estonia

My incles *Juhan,Villu* and

My Father in Estonia

Mother 3 yrs. Old

Mother as young girl.

My Mother in Estonia 1931

Mother, I and my Sister

Reval 21/01/1944

I, Mother and my Sister in Merikula, Narva

Mother in Estonia pre 1944

Mother my Sister and I

Estonian winter

House we shared in Deshingen,

near Ingolstadt, Germany

I and a friend wearing borrowed

Estonian Folk costume, Deshingen

Mother and I holding my brother

Austria 1945

My passport photo 1950